"Carra has created a book that is a treasure to carry around in your pocket, your car, next to your heart. And when your life gets stressful or overwhelming, pull out this book and open to any page. Even if it doesn't directly apply, it will put you back to that centered place where you can act and live."

Joan Darling,
Emmy Award™ *winning director*

"Not just for Actors, this book is for anyone who strives to live a more balanced, centered, creative life."

David Weisberg,
Screenplay writer 'Double Jeopardy', 'The Rock'

"A great piece of work that will speak to many people on various levels. The masses will be reached in metaphoric terms. Ms. Robertson is offering important lessons of life with a common sense approach. Her wisdom is straightforward and as she states it best, "Simplicity is the key." This is a help-filled book dealing with creative balance, centering points and appropriate solutions."

Maxine Rockmaker Day, Ph.D.,
Marriage and Family Therapist/Mediator

D1557158

MEDITATIONS FOR ACTORS

MEDITATIONS FOR ACTORS
for the actor within us all

CARRA ROBERTSON

DABLOND
LOS ANGELES

Published by:
DABLOND
8391 Beverly Blvd.
PMB #189
Los Angeles, CA 90048
(888)387-1477.
www.DABLOND.com

Cover design by Kelly Grief
FIRST EDITION

Library of Congress Catalog Card Number: 00-090361

ISBN 0-9679837-0-3

To my daughter, Alexandra, and to my sister, Gina, both of whom embody joy and the wonder of life.

FOREWORD

Some years ago, I wrote a book entitled, *Free To Act*. At that time, I had already trained some 40,000 actors and actresses in the Warren Robertson Theatre Workshop and was considered one of the most significant teachers in the profession. My book was designed to help actors realize that they are rare instruments of expression that need care and require tending, similar to that of a violin or any other fine instrument. The human instrument is of such complexity, not only in the playing of it, but also in its relation to its world of existence. Hence, all of the scientific philosophies and spiritual understandings that are available can contribute greatly to the evolution and fulfillment of a talent.

Too many potential talents and even many acknowledged ones have ended prematurely or tragically because of this lack of understanding of SELF and the world it inhabits. Carra Robertson is an accomplished actress, coach and playwright and whom like all great teachers, remains an avid student of all that is available toward greater knowledge of this mystery called SELF.

In this book, Carra has beautifully composed this knowledge into understandable and applicable exercises and examples that can contribute immensely to the actor's craft and to the life that nurtures and supports it. I recommend it highly.

WARREN ROBERTSON

ACKNOWLEDGMENTS

There are two people who have been essential in helping me to see this project to publication: Kelly Grief, for his unconditional love and support and encouraging the vision of completion; and my dear friend Allyson Adams for her assistance and creative inspiration.

In addition, I would like to thank my mother Gail, my sister, Gina, my father, Warren, and my friend, Gregory Phelan, whose nurturing and fortitude have all been outstanding and gratefully appreciated.

Thank you to Roddy Wilson for helping me hone in on the topic for this book and to Anne Wilson Schaef for her kindness, wisdom and her inspiring written words.

Other dear hearts who I must also thank are: Lorin and Jerry Biederman, Joan Darling, Maxine Rockmaker Day, David Weisberg, James Bonnet, and of course, all my students and all my teachers.

TABLE OF CONTENTS

INTRODUCTION

Originally, this project began as a self-help book intended specifically for actors. Over the years, I have noticed that actors, whether successful or not, have constantly faced the struggle of balancing their personal lives with their professional. The pursuit and maintenance of a career in the field of acting requires relentless and unwavering attention. I wanted to create a handbook that would help ground the actor both on and off the stage. However, as I began developing the chapters, it became apparent that the information I wanted to convey actually applied to a much broader sector of the population than just those who were Hollywood or Broadway bound.

I found that when we examine ourselves, no matter what vocation we practice, no matter how we look physically, or even how shy we may feel, *there lies a bit of an actor within us all.* Whether it be entertaining our friends by telling jokes, delivering a presentation at a work meeting, costuming ourselves for a night out on the town, or simply and sadly, masking our feelings so we can get through the day, we basically employ at least one of an actor's many skills in our everyday life.

Hence, I realized that this book can be useful to just about anyone.

Each chapter is entitled with a theme. I then offer a quote that may provoke some thoughtful insight relative to that theme. The actual meditation follows, which I have kept succinct, knowing that reading time is often limited. It would be my hope that you would allow yourself the luxury of time *afterward*. Give your brain and your being ample opportunity to digest what you have read. This way, you can process the information at your own pace. No pressure should be put on yourself to "get it" right away, or even at all, for that matter. Depending on where we are in our lives, certain things affect us differently and our perspective alters. It is for this reason that I suggest going back to particular chapters weeks or even months after you have originally visited them. Chances are, they may take on a whole new meaning for you.

As you'll notice in the meditations, I employ the term "actor" as my focal character. Once again, please know that I am referring to "the actor in us all" as well as the professional thespian. Also, some of the phraseology I use can be partial to the acting field, but I believe you can use it as a metaphor for the elements that surround *your* particular life circumstances.

To complete each meditation, I offer a sentence or two that you may use as an affirmation. I have also included an extra page at the end of each chapter, designated "notes", so that you may have a space to jot down some thoughts of your own.

Toward the end of the book, I added a section entitled, "On the theme of...". This can be a quick, flip-open-to-the-page section where you may easily choose a special theme for your day.

My desire is that the material in this book proves to be helpful as a grounding tool as well as a reminder of our unique connection to creativity, harmony and greatness.

COMMUNICATION

symbol = to speak

"You and I ought not to die before we have explained ourselves to each other."

-John Adams

In order to best communicate, we need to express ourselves in the most universal way possible. That is, when we use our body, gestures, facial expressions, we can be understood by those who do not even speak the same language. And as actors, when we do speak, we must remember to enunciate and verbalize with clarity.

As for the choices we make in a scene, no matter how mundane or "bread and butter" the writing seems, we must choose intentions, actions, objectives (whatever term suits you best), with the highest stakes possible. Writers employ particular words for a reason. We must honor the material as actors by deciding that the choices we make are real, strong, and crucially important. That is not to say that every scene needs to be played with the intensity of life and death, but nothing the author has offered should be taken for granted or be considered too lightly.

Ideally, words would never be wasted and all that we did speak, we would make worthwhile.

**WHEN I EXPRESS MYSELF, IT MATTERS.
I CHERISH THE ABILITY
TO COMMUNICATE CLEARLY.**

NOTES

PREPARATION

symbol = to anticipate in the mind

"Nothing is more dangerous than an idea, when you have only one idea."

-Alain

In order for us to achieve our potential, we must be willing to relinquish any preconceived ideas we have of ourselves or of our performance once it is show time.

Absolutely we need to prepare by making choices. During rehearsal, the director may adore our ideas. In the best of all possible worlds, he/she can help us build upon them, making the endeavor a true collaboration. But even in an ideal case, we must remain open to variation, modification and even alteration. However, if we present our interpretation and the director envisions something quite different, we have to at least try an alternative, letting go of our original intention.

Oftentimes we engage ourselves so completely in one mindset, that it prohibits the flow of other things to magnetize toward us. Holding on too tightly to only one philosophy of thought can close the door to other possibilities that may allow for brilliant change to our performance and to our lives.

Part of true preparation is to be prepared for what we could not possibly have prepared ourselves for. Expect the unexpected. By allowing for the possibility that more exists beyond one pre-conceived idea, we open ourselves to a richer rehearsal process as well as performance.

I RELINQUISH MY FEAR OF CHANGE.
I EXERCISE MY CREATIVITY
WITH COURAGE.

NOTES

DILIGENCE

symbol = to step with determination/
to progress

"It is better to wear out than rust out."
                    --Bishop Richard Cumberland

Acting is a muscle. It has memory, thrives with practice, and if unused, can atrophy. Our craft requires the same maintenance as an athlete's body. We must tend to it with regularity and care.

If we wait for someone to give us a job in order to exercise our acting muscle, we are doing ourselves a great disservice. Oftentimes, weeks or months go by between bookings and even then, the opportunity to really explore our craft on the job does not necessarily exist. This is especially true for television. It is rare that much consideration is given to the "acting" portion of that medium due to time restraints and tight budgets. Even in studio-made films the rehearsal time is quite limited, if it even exists. Sometimes in independent filmmaking, more attention and time are allocated to the actor, as it is in many theatre productions. But even then, with the unfortunate high price tag attached to theatre space these days, the romantic ideal of extensive rehearsals periods is becoming less of a reality.

As is true in any profession, if we love our craft, we want to practice it as much as possible. Take a class, produce a play, start a group. Never mind the fact that very few casting directors would go to bat for you on a job if you seemed rusty at the audition. Would you hire a doctor to remove your tonsils who hasn't seen a patient in thirteen years? Would you hire a band for your wedding who has only practiced once in a basement apartment? Delight in creating opportunities to explore your work and all of its creativity.

**I AM EMPOWERED BY PRACTICE.
MY SPIRIT IS REJUVENATED
BY TAKING ACTION.**

NOTES

GROUNDING

symbol = to stand upright/
feet firmly planted

"Everyone journeys through character as well as through time. The person one becomes depends on the person one has been."

-Dick Francis

Once in a while there are moments, (mostly at the beginning of a scene), in which we cannot quite settle in. We feel disjointed, separated from our intentions and sometimes from our bodies. Our nerves and our minds distract us from present circumstances. The words come out but they are disconnected from anything real. We must remember to breathe and take a moment to regroup. It may feel like a tremendously long pause, but it really is not. Taking a mere five second break can help us to refocus and ground ourselves.

In some instances, we worry about what the audience is thinking while we are performing. This happens a lot at auditions. When we begin to judge the job we are doing, we question our choices and become insecure. Some of us react by disappearing, upstaging ourselves, mumbling or lowering our volume. Others do the opposite and try to compensate by "going over the top".

We do not trust that the groundwork we have laid is enough. So, we *yell* our lines, or *force* our emotions, or throw the nearest chair.

In order for our performances to be their most robust and effective, we must come from a place of calm, center, and strong footing. It is only from that core that we can begin to build and enhance the job that we do.

**THROUGH THE BREATH, I INTEGRATE MYSELF INTO THE VERY FOUNDATION ON WHICH I STAND.
I AM EMPOWERED BY MY STILLNESS.**

NOTES

CREATIVITY

symbol = paintbrush/ the tool from which
creativity flows

"If it moves, salute it; if it doesn't move, pick it up; and if you can't pick it up, paint it."
-Anonymous

When we are open and receptive with all of our senses, our unique creativity flows easily and vastly. On stage, things happen that we cannot plan. A phone rings, an actor forgets his lines, a glass breaks. We must acknowledge everything that is going on around us. The audience certainly does. To deny it would be a lie and the performance would be skewed.

Dealing with the unpredictable is what allows us to unleash our creative juices. Unforeseen obstacles are divine treats that give us an opportunity to *"act"* in our own artistic and unique fashion. Obviously, our actions must remain within the boundaries of the given circumstances of the scene. However, simply because an author did not write a specific behavior, does not mean it does not exist. We tend to discover the most interesting character behavior when we are faced with problem solving on the spot. We remedy the situation with creativity.

The only way we can recognize an obstacle, in order to utilize our creative skills, is to be aware and in the moment.

**I AM ALIGNED AND IN THE PRESENT.
I ALLOW MY DISTINCT SELF
TO RESPOND AND CREATE.**

NOTES

LAUGHTER

symbol = smiling from the heart

"When the first baby laughed for the first time, the laugh broke into a thousand pieces and they all went skipping about and that was the beginning of fairies."

-J.M. Barrie

Laughter is always appropriate. The manner in which we display it is the variable. Laughter is simply an emotion spawned by something our senses perceive to be funny. It could be brought on by something that makes us nervous, or by something that is driving us mad. It is a chemical response that acts as a release of energy that, for the most part, feels good. Granted, there are places and situations where laughing out loud may disturb others or cause offense. But chances are, we have learned to behave "acceptably" in public.

On stage however, actors sometimes forget they are human. *People have unpredictable responses.* Just because a scene denotes, "Couple is arguing", does not mean it is a scene about yelling. If an actor uses his senses to recall a time when he was in a particular verbal scrap, he might just remember that laughter actually sneaked its way in. We might giggle out of nervousness from being caught in a lie. We may chortle at a ridiculous accusation made against us.

In order to deliver the most genuine performance, we cannot ever rule out the possibility that laughter may become part of a scene. How it is *dealt with* and then *responded to*, (while most importantly keeping to the integrity of the material), adds more dimension to the situation and gives it a larger sense of reality.

On the flip side, just because a footnote may indicate, "He laughs sheepishly", does not mean the actor should falsely manufacture a chuckle. There is nothing more uncomfortable than watching someone fake laughter. It is unsettling. Unless the script absolutely requires that laughter is seen and heard, an actor is better off simply allowing the emotion that is occurring in the moment rather than forcing otherwise. However, if we are directed to laugh, we should approach the scene by making specific choices that create the laughter from an authentic place.

I WELCOME LAUGHTER IN MY LIFE. WHEN LAUGHTER FILLS MY BEING, I AM ON THE RIGHT PATH.

NOTES

APPREHENSION

symbol = to hide from experience

"We must travel in the direction of our fear."
                                                    -John Berryman

When we are fearful, what is the worst thing we can imagine? We have a *real* nervous breakdown in front of the camera or the audience? Our heads explode from frustration? Besides defying one of the main golden rules of acting and society, *"Never hurt yourself or another"*, pretty much anything goes. When we make our choices, remain within the context of the given circumstances, and then proceed steadfastly into the scene, whatever comes up creatively and/or emotionally is not only appropriate, but damn exciting. Being afraid of this type of powerful performance is robbing ourselves as well as the audience of a rich, unique experience.

Most of the time, the fear begins before even stepping on to the set. We must remember to watch our breath and our thoughts. Thinking can terrify us, especially when we exaggerate in our minds problems that do not even yet exist. Focussing on the breath can help to calm us. However, we cannot deny nor invalidate certain feelings and charges of energy in our bodies. The best thing to do is let them be. Bring yourself on stage with all that you are at that moment.

Venturing into uncharted psychological and emotional territory to fulfill the needs of our character can also cause us to have a mini-panic attack. We need not worry. Why be an actor if one is unwilling to explore the human psyche and all of its drama? We must have courage and take the ride of the character when we agree to do a particular role. Remember, it is "acting". We will not really become a cripple, or die, or be sent to an insane asylum. Our job is to re-create an event, depict in the third dimension behavior originated on a page, share with an audience our artistic interpretation of a story. We must move through our fear in order to be able to offer our best.

I ADDRESS MY FEAR.
MY COURAGE AND SUCCESS EVOLVE
FROM KNOWING THAT MY BEING
IS STRONGER THAN MY FEAR.

<u>NOTES</u>

EMOTIONS

symbol = passion

"They are ill discoverers that think there is no land, when they can see nothing but the sea."

-Francis Bacon

It takes a long time to trust that when we apply craft, skill, and practice to our performance that the *"work"* works. We do not always have to be feeling something in order for the audience to have pathos.

In some roles, for example, we may chose to cry during a certain section of a particular monologue. But if we have set ourselves up properly, that is, making specific choices about our character and his circumstances, the performance begins to take on a life of its own. Ultimately, it will not matter whether we actually cry. When this type of high art occurs, the emotions we display on stage are not always the ones we plan. Just as in life offstage, if tears do not fall from our eyes it does not necessarily mean there is a lack of sadness.

Sometimes it is more powerful when we allow the *audience* to cry for our character. The point is, we do not have to wail or emit tears to evoke sorrow, nor do we have to laugh to convey joy.

Actors need to be reminded that they are not required nor expected to constantly be emoting. Otherwise, we would be called "emotors" and "emotoresses". Our thoughts are not our emotions. Our feelings are not our emotions. The dictionary may equate these, but I beg to differ. Our emotions most logically seem to be *expressions* of our feelings, bursts of energy responding as a result of an internal experience. Also, that is not to say that these all go hand in hand. Oftentimes we have a strong feeling about something, but we do not necessarily exhibit an external display. If we actors are *"acting"* as if we are human, it would follow suit that we can actually have feelings, actually successfully convey them, yet never outwardly display an iota of emotion.

I AM ABLE TO COMMUNICATE IN MANY FORMS.
I TRUST ALTERNATIVES TO MY EMOTIONS IN ORDER TO CONVEY MY MESSAGE.

NOTES

CRITICISM

symbol = to humble oneself

"Opinion is a flitting thing, but truth outlasts the sun."

-Emily Dickinson

If we listen to the good reviews, then we must also listen to the bad. For the most part, it is difficult to trust from others what may or may not be an accurate account of our performance. Then who is to say what is the truth? We are! The actor knows the truth.

If we tell the truth on stage, we can never do a bad job. Our performances will always be believable. We may need direction or advice on how to improve, but at least we will be interesting to watch and we will not be phony.

Criticism is always derived from opinion. Some critiques can prove to be productive when offered by those whose opinion we admire. The times we should be wary of review is when the words are spoken or written by someone who has an agenda, may be jealous, wants your job, may dislike the character, or simply does not have a clue. Again, we are the only ones who truly know if our performance was delivered with truth and integrity. If we did not do our best, we usually know it. If that be the case, we can forgive ourselves and vow to improve by committing fully the next time.

However, if we succeed at what we set out to do and know the truth in our body, mind, and spirit, nothing anyone says or writes can disturb us. All we can feel is pleased.

I KNOW MY OWN TRUTH.
I AM OPEN AND RECEPTIVE
TO INFORMATION THAT IS HELPFUL .

NOTES

IN THE MOMENT

symbol = body, mind + soul

"The past is history, the future is a mystery, and this moment is a gift. That is why this moment is called 'the present'."

-Unknown

True performance can only occur in the moment. Character choices and intentions are consciously made before arriving on stage. That is our homework. However, once the curtain rises we must trust that our groundwork has been laid, and in a sense, let it all go. All we need to do is show up. If we are aware and receptive as to what is occurring in the moment, things we never could have imagined or planned will begin to happen. Our scenes will become richer for the audience as well as for ourselves.

If we are stuck in our heads and all we hear is our ongoing commentary, (which is usually judgmental), we could not possibly be present. Our thoughts are distractions from the present time. When we are in the moment, we acknowledge our thoughts and simply watch them pass by. There is no time to stop and engage ourselves in a conversation with these musings.

Being in the moment allows us to respond spontaneously and uniquely. It gives our performance an authentic dimension comparable to no other. The most brilliant performances are the ones in which the actor is fully present sensorially and spiritually.

I TAKE IN THE TEMPERATURE OF THE ROOM. I LISTEN TO THE SOUNDS.
I SMELL THE AIR.
I EXAMINE MY HEART.
ALL I AM IS HERE NOW.

NOTES

ACTION

symbol = to journey as a means of
discovery, progress, and self-expression

"We know what happens to people who stay in the middle of the road. They get run down."

-Aneurin Bevan

"Even if you're on the right track, you'll get run over if you just sit there."

-Will Rogers

Action is propelled by a motive, an incentive. We must define our need in order to be incited to "act". When we make a move, whether it be emotional, verbal, or physical, it is because we have a need or desire to reach a goal. Motivation spawns the action. If our character is in prison, for example, and we are thirsty, our motivation would be to quench the thirst. Now we have a reason for pleading with the guard, or getting up and pouring a glass, or licking the raindrops off the small portion of windowsill. Those are the actions we may take.

When we find ourselves in limbo, unable to take action, it is simply because we have not yet defined for ourselves *what* is motivating our character or *why*. We get stuck because we have not found a good enough reason to move forward. There is no incentive. We must discover the "because", the reason, the need the character has to achieve something, in order for us to "act", to take action with authenticity.

What are our given circumstances? Once we are clear about those facts, we can begin to explore *what* it is that we want. Once we identify *what* we want, *what* our needs are, we can make choices about how to go and get it. Making decisions about *how* to go about getting these things will justify *why* we do what we do.

As in our world offstage, we need to assess our existing circumstances. From there, we can begin to identify our goals, desires, and needs. It is then that we can clearly choose actions that will assist us in our achievement.

**I FOCUS ON MY NEEDS AND DESIRES.
MY THOUGHTS AND MY ACTIONS
ASSIST ME IN MANIFESTING
MY DESIRED REALITY.**

NOTES

REASONING

symbol = to examine a point of view/
to see farther

"If it was so, it might be; and if it were so, it would be; but as it isn't, it ain't."

-Lewis Carroll

We can only rely upon our present circumstances in order for us to remain as focused as possible. Worrying about what does not yet exist or may *never* exist, is basically asking for unneeded anxiety and distraction. On or offstage, we are led astray from our productive path when we perseverate on things that are simply irrelevant to what is occurring in "the now".

When we ask "what if" type questions, we are creating circumstances for ourselves that are not yet real nor ever may be. *What if I forget my lines? What if I win the lottery? What if no one shows up?* As an exercise in imagination, it can be challenging to explore the potential of a situation, even when we explore it to absurdity. However, it is important to remember that "what if" is merely that. "If", by its very own nature is only a possibility, not even a probability. Most of the "ifs" are variables that we could never anticipate or prepare for anyway. Hence, if we are not looking to play a mind game with ourselves, indulging in "what if" can be a waste of time.

It would stand to reason then, that by simply accepting and dealing with the absolute given circumstances, we can enjoy each moment in its pureness and offer a performance that is available and real.

I RELINQUISH MY FEAR OF THE UNKNOWN.
I ALLOW WHAT EXISTS IN THIS MOMENT TO BE MY PRIMARY FOCUS.

NOTES

REGRET

symbol= mind disturbed by act of passion/
shame

"Never should on yourself"

-Unknown

    We are our toughest critics. We must keep that in mind so we do not punish ourselves too harshly.

    When we make a choice, it can never be right or wrong. What it is, is simply a commitment to a particular direction. Sometimes, it may not be the inclination that a director envisions. In an audition situation, it may not be the way a casting director would like to see the scene. In some cases, they will appreciate our effort, explain that they would prefer a different choice, and then give us another opportunity. If so, carry on without giving thought to, "I *should* have done that first", or "I knew *I should have* (anything)".

    As thinking creatures, we must always take responsibility for our actions. Sometimes we do not behave wisely. Nonetheless, everything we do, we at one point, *decided* to do. At that time of decision making, we made an agreement with ourselves that this would be our course of action. At that time, we made those choices and thought them to be the best. So how then can we reprimand ourselves or feel regretful when we are displeased with the results?

We can sometimes feel disappointed. But forget about castigating ourselves. For the health of our future decisions as well as our performances, we can only look forward. Regret is a waste of time and a tremendous insult to our being.

When we fully trust our instincts, we stop setting ourselves up for *"shoulds"*. Unless we have consciously and purposely sabotaged our performance, (or a relationship, or a certain situation), regret is useless and does not have a space in our well being.

I COMMEND MY TRUST IN MYSELF.
I ACCEPT THE RESULTS OF MY DECISIONS WITHOUT MISGIVINGS.

NOTES

CLEMENCY

symbol = having a conscience/
able to relate/forgive

"Please do not shoot the pianist. He's doing his best."

-Anonymous

As an audience member, we must employ forgiveness every once in a while for what occurs on stage. Either an actor does not know any better, has been misled by a clueless director, or simply is having a horribly bad day. Rarely does an actor purposely set out to do a lousy job. It is for this reason, we must find it within ourselves to have compassion for the performer. Let us not pity, but rather empathize, knowing it may be us up there one day stinking up the stage.

When we are cast along with another actor whom we feel does not share the same caliber of experience or skill, we cannot dwell upon these feelings. Whatever we believe about our co-workers, we must not let it interfere with our own performance. That is not to say that we should compromise our actions in order to meet their current standards. But rather, when viewed through humble eyes, it can be a gift of generosity if we do our best work as an example to which others may aspire.

When, in the unfortunate event, it is we who are not up to par or are not delivering the goods of the scene, we must first take a step back and examine the situation with objectivity. Next, we must have mercy on ourselves. Harping on the negative will not offer a solution. We must forgive ourselves and move forward. Is our instrument rusty, thus requiring more acting workouts? Do we need more rehearsal time? Does the character require more research? Do we mistrust the director and feel lost? Look within and explore all of your questions.

I AM A SUCCESSFUL PROBLEM SOLVER WHEN I AM FREE OF JUDGEMENT. WHEN I FORGIVE, I MOVE FORWARD.

NOTES

HABIT

symbol = to drag oneself along
again and again

"Habit is a great deadener."

-Samuel Beckett

There is a fine line between constructive practice and habit. When our response is automatic because we are used to doing the same thing over and over, it is generally done unconsciously. This is habit. It is like an involuntary mode of behavior we have acquired through somewhat mindless repetition.

When we are acting, or taking action in our lives, we absolutely want to use the knowledge we have accumulated through studies or from previous experiences. That requires wherewithal as well as receptivity to possible change. It would seem wise then, that we would want to steer clear of doing anything habitually. In order to maintain a freshness about our performance, we would not want to behave blindly. It is imperative that even if we are doing the same role for the eighty-fifth time, we rejoice in our awareness, challenge ourselves, keep our minds and instincts spry. We can still make similar choices over and over, but the key is to do it consciously and preferably with a different outlook and perspective each time.

On stage, a good habit is to not develop any habits. We never want to take our craft for granted, potentially causing stale performances.

I VALUE PRACTICE AND REPETITION. DISTINCTIVELY, EVERYTHING ALIVE EVOLVES FROM ONE MOMENT TO THE NEXT.

NOTES

CLARITY

symbol = one who is clear with wisdom

"I am not at all the sort of person you and I took me for."

-Jane Carlyle

Some of us have grand misconceptions about who we actually are and how we present ourselves to the world. At times, we are so concerned with labeling ourselves as "this kind of person" or "that type" that we leave ourselves no room for dimension or further self-discovery. As actors, it is crucially important to allow all parts of our being to emerge. The only way to begin to do so is by accepting that we may be more than we think we are. And in some cases, less.

Judgement must be left behind. There is no place for comment when creating a character. If, for example, an actor finds loud, boisterous people extremely obnoxious, the actor may not commit to those characteristics for fear of appearing too unappealing. Forget the label. What are the qualities, mannerisms and behavior patterns of the character? Who is to say that the actor does not already embody these characteristics and does not want to admit it? As the performer, we must uninhibitedly allow parts of our private selves to be displayed. After all, there is no one on stage as that character but ourselves.

Perhaps, for example, our nature is outgoing and gregarious but we have been given the part of a character who is incredibly shy. There are several ways to approach this. However, the most powerful choice, (that is, one that comes from an authentic place), would be to tap into the timid essence within ourselves. We are all vulnerable beings. We might just discover that we actually are shy and side-step our fear by being loud or overly-friendly or by using alcohol or narcotics. The ability to tap into our vulnerability is an invaluable skill onstage and off. It is the core of what allows us to shine.

The clearer we become about our abilities, sensibilities, and our vast pool of behavioral knowledge, the more accurate our portrayals will become.

I AM A COMPLEX BEING RECEPTIVE TO SEEING MYSELF MORE CLEARLY. WITHOUT JUDGEMENT, I ACCEPT WHO I AM.

NOTES

LESS IS MORE

symbol = simply oneself

"He more had pleased us, had he pleased us less."
-Joseph Addison

Wardrobe, makeup, sets, props, accents, limps, and twitches are just a few of the wonderful designs we employ. However, the object of using these accessories is to enhance our performance, not steal it. We must remember that use of these aides must be used with integrity and moderation. Our performance can become horribly unfocused when we try to "do" too many things at once. Simplicity is the key.

When we are prepared and have a message to communicate, we are heard more profoundly the more honestly and subtly we express ourselves.

I AVOID PUSHING.
WHO I AM IS ENOUGH.

NOTES

Action

MOVEMENT WITHOUT INTENTION DOES NOT
EQUAL ACTION. I PROPEL MYSELF FORWARD
WHEN I HAVE A FOCUS.

Success

I UNDERSTAND THAT THE REWARDS OF SUCCESS
ARRIVE IN MANY DIFFERENT FORMS. IT IS ONLY
THROUGH ACTION THAT I ACHIEVE SUCCESS.

Discipline

REMEMBERING WHAT I DESIRE KEEPS ME
FOCUSED.

Courage

ONE ACT OF COURAGE INFLUENCES THE
OUTCOME OF MY PERFORMANCE, MY DAY, AND
PERHAPS MY LIFE.

Longevity

I ACCEPT CHALLENGE AS A MEANS OF
EVOLUTION. I MUST CONTINUE TO EVOLVE
IN ORDER TO KEEP MY CAREER AND MY LIFE
FRESH.

Exercise

DAILY I EXERCISE MY MIND, CRAFT, AND BODY
FOR OPTIMAL WELL-BEING.

Reflection

I EXAMINE MY THOUGHTS AND BEHAVIOR.
WITHOUT JUDGEMENT, I MAINTAIN THOSE
QUALITIES WHICH ENHANCE MY PERFORMANCE.
IN TURN, I SHED THOSE THAT DO ME A
DISSERVICE.

Knowledge

I POSSESS ABUNDANT INNATE KNOWLEDGE.
I AM OPEN TO BEING REMINDED.

Merit

OF ALL THE GOOD THAT I RECEIVE, I AM
DESERVED. I AM OPEN TO ACCEPT.

❧❧❧

Winning

I STRIVE TO OVERCOME MY LIMITATIONS.
RECOGNITION FROM OTHERS OR THE LACK
THEREOF, WILL NOT DISTRACT ME FROM MY
GOALS.

❧❧❧

Instincts

I TRUST THAT MY GUTERAL SENSATIONS ARE
ACCURATE. WHEN I BEHAVE INSTINCTIVELY, I
AM TRUE TO MYSELF AND MY HIGHEST PATH.

❧❧❧

Presence

WITHOUT FEAR, I FACE MY INHIBITIONS.
I ALLOW ALL OF MY UNIQUE SELF TO SHINE.

Complexity

I RECOGNIZE THAT MY WORK AND
MY RELATIONSHIPS MAY BE COMPLEX.
I AM SOOTHED WHEN I AM REMINDED THAT
THEY ARE INTRICATE ENTITIES
MERELY COMPRISED OF MANY SIMPLE PARTS.

Completion

WHEN I FOLLOW THROUGH *COMPLETELY* WITH
MY HEARTFELT INTENTIONS, I AM SATISFIED.
REWARD GREATLY LIES IN COMPLETION,
REGARDLESS OF OUTCOME.

BIBLIOGRAPHY

Carlson, Richard. *Don't Sweat the Small Stuff.* New York: Hyperion, 1997.

Chopra, Deepak. *The Seven Spiritual Laws of Success.* San Rafael, California: New World Library, 1994.

de Mello, Anthony. *Awareness.* New York: Doubleday, 1992.

Hagen, Uta. *Respect for Acting.* New York: Macmillan, 1973.

Neumann, Erich. *Art and the Creative Unconscious.* New York: Bollingen/Pantheon, 1959.

Robertson, Warren. *Free To Act.* New York: G.P. Putnam's Sons, 1978.

Roman, Sanaya. *Creating Money.* Tiburon, California: HJ Kramer Inc, 1988.

Schaef, Anne Wilson. *Meditations for Women Who Do Too Much*. New York: HarperCollins, 1990.

Stanislavski, Constantin. *An Actor Prepares.* New York: Theatre Arts Book, 1964.

INDEX

feeling 34,35
focus 18,31,50,51,73

Goals 25,26,39,40
grounding 18,19,20

Habit 61,62,63

Instinct 63,75
intention 6,10,73
in the moment 23,41,42,43,51

Judgment 42,66,67,74

Knowledge 67,74

Laughter 25,26,27
less is more 69
longevity 74

Moderation 71
motivation 46,47

Practice 14,15,34,63
preparation 9,10,11
presence 41,75

Reasoning 49
receptive, receptivity 22,39,42,62,67

For ordering
"Meditations for Actors":

DABLOND
8391 Beverly Blvd. PMB#189
Los Angeles, CA 90048
(888)387-1477

Website: www.DABLOND.com

A NOTE FROM THE AUTHOR

I am always open to feedback and would love to hear any inspiring thoughts you may have. If you have an affirmation or meditation that you created yourself, I encourage you to send it and perhaps we can all compile an enhanced edition in the future. Thanks for reading!
You may write to me in care of/ DABLOND or E-mail me at Carra@DABLOND.com

Carra Robertson